DoN't Be a GOAT aNd Fill YOUR NaMe HeRe:

____

____

So, if somebody finds it, he could call:

____

DO YOU READY tO PUT YOUR FINANCES IN ORDER AND CLEAN UP tHE MESS? LET'S GOAT!

Instructions:

First of all – congratulation on your decision to start keeping your money under control.

I know – it's not easy. Tell me about it...

But it seems that the time is already came.

So, follow this simple instructions and you will find out that it's not so complicated after all.

1.   Write on your cheklist and expences log regurarly!
2.   Don´t cheat!
3.   Be firm and strict.

This is it!

To have it on paper, all the time in your pocket is better than any mobile app. Some could say it´s an old school, but I say: baaaaaa – they don´t goat it!

MONTHLY BUDGET WORKSHEET

MONTH: YEAR:

Starting debt

MONTHLY INCOME
1 SOURCE:
2 SOURCE:

3 SOURCE:
4 SOURCE:

5 SOURCE:

TOTAL:

EXPENSES	SPENT
Rent/Mortgage	
Electric	
Water	
Phone/Cell	
Internet	
Health insurance	
Life insurance	
Car insurance	
Gas/Other transport	
Car payment	
Gifts/Books/Cosmetic	
Cloths	
Entertainment	
Eating out	
Groceries	
Utilities	
Pets	
Charity	
Unexpected	
Savings	
TOTAL:	

MONTHLY INCOME

-

TOTAL EXPENSES

=

TOTAL left to apply to debts

Debts	Applied amount	Still Owe
______	______	______
______	______	______
______	______	______
______	______	______
______	______	______
______	______	______
______	______	______
______	______	______
______	______	______
______	______	______
______	______	______

TOTAL debt:

WEEKLY "WHERE'S MY MONEY" PART

MONDAY:

	Need it?	AMOUNT
_______	Yes / No	_______
_______	Yes / No	_______
_______	Yes / No	_______
_______	Yes / No	_______
_______	Yes / No	_______
_______	Yes / No	_______

TUESDAY:

	Need it?	AMOUNT
_______	Yes / No	_______
_______	Yes / No	_______
_______	Yes / No	_______
_______	Yes / No	_______
_______	Yes / No	_______
_______	Yes / No	_______

WEDNESDAY:

	Need it?	AMOUNT
_______	Yes / No	_______
_______	Yes / No	_______
_______	Yes / No	_______
_______	Yes / No	_______
_______	Yes / No	_______
_______	Yes / No	_______

EXPENSES:

INCOME   1 SOURCE: 2 SOURCE: 3 SOURCE:

Thursday:

	Need it?		Amount
____________________	Yes	No	__________
____________________	Yes	No	__________
____________________	Yes	No	__________
____________________	Yes	No	__________
____________________	Yes	No	__________
____________________	Yes	No	__________

Friday:

	Need it?		Amount
____________________	Yes	No	__________
____________________	Yes	No	__________
____________________	Yes	No	__________
____________________	Yes	No	__________
____________________	Yes	No	__________
____________________	Yes	No	__________

Weekend:

	Need it?		Amount
____________________	Yes	No	__________
____________________	Yes	No	__________
____________________	Yes	No	__________
____________________	Yes	No	__________
____________________	Yes	No	__________
____________________	Yes	No	__________

Total weekly Expenses:

Income   4 Source: 5 Source: 6 Source:

weekly "where's my money" part

MONDAY:

Need it?		AMOUNT
Yes	No	
Yes	No	
Yes	No	
Yes	No	
Yes	No	
Yes	No	

TUESDAY:

Need it?		AMOUNT
Yes	No	
Yes	No	
Yes	No	
Yes	No	
Yes	No	
Yes	No	

WEDNESDAY:

Need it?		AMOUNT
Yes	No	
Yes	No	
Yes	No	
Yes	No	
Yes	No	
Yes	No	

EXPENSES:

INCOME   1 SOURCE: 2 SOURCE: 3 SOURCE:

Thursday:

	Need it?		Amount
____________________	Yes	No	__________
____________________	Yes	No	__________
____________________	Yes	No	__________
____________________	Yes	No	__________
____________________	Yes	No	__________
____________________	Yes	No	__________

Friday:

	Need it?		Amount
____________________	Yes	No	__________
____________________	Yes	No	__________
____________________	Yes	No	__________
____________________	Yes	No	__________
____________________	Yes	No	__________
____________________	Yes	No	__________

Weekend:

	Need it?		Amount
____________________	Yes	No	__________
____________________	Yes	No	__________
____________________	Yes	No	__________
____________________	Yes	No	__________
____________________	Yes	No	__________
____________________	Yes	No	__________

Total weekly Expenses:

Income   4 Source: 5 Source: 6 Source:

weekly "where's my money" part

MONDAY:

	Need it?		AMOUNT
_______________	Yes	No	_______
_______________	Yes	No	_______
_______________	Yes	No	_______
_______________	Yes	No	_______
_______________	Yes	No	_______
_______________	Yes	No	_______

TUESDAY:

	Need it?		AMOUNT
_______________	Yes	No	_______
_______________	Yes	No	_______
_______________	Yes	No	_______
_______________	Yes	No	_______
_______________	Yes	No	_______
_______________	Yes	No	_______

WednesDAY:

	Need it?		AMOUNT
_______________	Yes	No	_______
_______________	Yes	No	_______
_______________	Yes	No	_______
_______________	Yes	No	_______
_______________	Yes	No	_______
_______________	Yes	No	_______

EXpenses:

INCOME   1 SOURCE: 2 SOURCE: 3 SOURCE:

THURSDAY:

Need it?   AMOUNT

____

- Yes / No
- Yes / No
- Yes / No
- Yes / No
- Yes / No
- Yes / No

FRIDAY:

Need it?   AMOUNT

____

- Yes / No
- Yes / No
- Yes / No
- Yes / No
- Yes / No
- Yes / No

WEEKEND:

Need it?   AMOUNT

____

- Yes / No
- Yes / No
- Yes / No
- Yes / No
- Yes / No
- Yes / No

Total weekly Expenses:

INCOME   4 SOURCE: 5 SOURCE: 6 SOURCE:

weekly "where's my money" part

MONDAY:

	Need it?		AMOUNT
______________	Yes	No	
______________	Yes	No	______________
______________	Yes	No	
______________	Yes	No	______________
______________	Yes	No	
______________	Yes	No	______________

TUESDAY:

	Need it?		AMOUNT
______________	Yes	No	
______________	Yes	No	______________
______________	Yes	No	
______________	Yes	No	______________
______________	Yes	No	
______________	Yes	No	______________

WEDNESDAY:

	Need it?		AMOUNT
______________	Yes	No	
______________	Yes	No	______________
______________	Yes	No	
______________	Yes	No	______________
______________	Yes	No	
______________	Yes	No	______________

EXPENSES:

INCOME   1 SOURCE: 2 SOURCE: 3 SOURCE:

THURSDAY:

Need it?   AMOUNT

Yes	No
Yes	No
Yes	No
Yes	No
Yes	No
Yes	No

FRIDAY:

Need it?   AMOUNT

Yes	No
Yes	No
Yes	No
Yes	No
Yes	No
Yes	No

WEEKEND:

Need it?   AMOUNT

Yes	No
Yes	No
Yes	No
Yes	No
Yes	No
Yes	No

TOTAL WEEKLY EXPENSES:

INCOME   4 SOURCE: 5 SOURCE: 6 SOURCE:

weekly "where's my money" part

MONDAY:

	Need it?	AMOUNT
_______________	Yes / No	_______
_______________	Yes / No	_______
_______________	Yes / No	_______
_______________	Yes / No	_______
_______________	Yes / No	_______
_______________	Yes / No	_______

TUESDAY:

	Need it?	AMOUNT
_______________	Yes / No	_______
_______________	Yes / No	_______
_______________	Yes / No	_______
_______________	Yes / No	_______
_______________	Yes / No	_______
_______________	Yes / No	_______

WEDNESDAY:

	Need it?	AMOUNT
_______________	Yes / No	_______
_______________	Yes / No	_______
_______________	Yes / No	_______
_______________	Yes / No	_______
_______________	Yes / No	_______
_______________	Yes / No	_______

EXPENSES:

INCOME   1 SOURCE: 2 SOURCE: 3 SOURCE:

THURSDAY:

____

____

____

____

Need it?

Yes No
Yes No
Yes No
Yes No
Yes No
Yes No

AMOUNT

____

____

____

____

FRIDAY:

____

____

____

____

Need it?

Yes No
Yes No
Yes No
Yes No
Yes No
Yes No

AMOUNT

____

____

____

____

WEEKEND:

____

____

____

____

Need it?

Yes No
Yes No
Yes No
Yes No
Yes No
Yes No

AMOUNT

____

____

____

____

TOTAL WEEKLY EXPENSES:

INCOME   4 SOURCE: 5 SOURCE: 6 SOURCE:

WRite some important Notes HeRe:

MONtHly budget WORksHeet

MONtH: YeaR:

Starting debt	

MONtHly INCOme
1 SOURCE:
2 SOURCE:

3 SOURCE:
4 SOURCE:

5 SOURCE:

TOTal:

Expenses	Spent
Rent/Mortgage	
Electric	
Water	
Phone/Cell	
Internet	
Health insurance	
Life insurance	
Car insurance	
Gas/Other transport	
Car payment	
Gifts/Books/Cosmetic	
Cloths	
Entertainment	
Eating out	
Groceries	
Utilities	
Pets	
Charity	
Unexpected	
Savings	
TOTal:	

MONtHly INCOme

−

TOTal expenses

=

TOTal left to apply to debts

Debts	Applied Amount	Still Owe
______	______	______
______	______	______
______	______	______
______	______	______
______	______	______
______	______	______
______	______	______
______	______	______
______	______	______
______	______	______
______	______	______
______	______	______

TOTal debt:

Weekly "Where's my money" Part

Monday:

Need it?   Amount

Yes   No
Yes   No
Yes   No
Yes   No
Yes   No
Yes   No

Tuesday:

Need it?   Amount

Yes   No
Yes   No
Yes   No
Yes   No
Yes   No
Yes   No

Wednesday:

Need it?   Amount

Yes   No
Yes   No
Yes   No
Yes   No
Yes   No
Yes   No

Expenses:

Income   1 Source: 2 Source: 3 Source:

THURSDAY:

Need it?	AMOUNT
Yes No	
Yes No	
Yes No	
Yes No	
Yes No	
Yes No	

FRIDAY:

Need it?	AMOUNT
Yes No	
Yes No	
Yes No	
Yes No	
Yes No	
Yes No	

WEEKEND:

Need it?	AMOUNT
Yes No	
Yes No	
Yes No	
Yes No	
Yes No	
Yes No	

Total weekly Expenses:

INCOME   4 SOURCE: 5 SOURCE: 6 SOURCE:

weekly "where's my money" part

MONDAY:

	Need it?	AMOUNT
____________	Yes No	________
____________	Yes No	________
____________	Yes No	________
____________	Yes No	________
____________	Yes No	________
____________	Yes No	________

TUESDAY:

	Need it?	AMOUNT
____________	Yes No	________
____________	Yes No	________
____________	Yes No	________
____________	Yes No	________
____________	Yes No	________
____________	Yes No	________

WEDNESDAY:

	Need it?	AMOUNT
____________	Yes No	________
____________	Yes No	________
____________	Yes No	________
____________	Yes No	________
____________	Yes No	________
____________	Yes No	________

EXPENSES:

INCOME   1 SOURCE: 2 SOURCE: 3 SOURCE:

THURSDAY: Need it?   AMOUNT

	Yes	No	
	Yes	No	
	Yes	No	
	Yes	No	
	Yes	No	
	Yes	No	

FRIDAY: Need it?   AMOUNT

	Yes	No	
	Yes	No	
	Yes	No	
	Yes	No	
	Yes	No	
	Yes	No	

WEEKEND: Need it?   AMOUNT

	Yes	No	
	Yes	No	
	Yes	No	
	Yes	No	
	Yes	No	
	Yes	No	

TOTAL WEEKLY EXPENSES:

INCOME   4 SOURCE: 5 SOURCE: 6 SOURCE:

Weekly "Where's My Money" Part

MONDAY: | | **Need it?** | | **AMOUNT**

________		Yes	No	________
________		Yes	No	________
________		Yes	No	________
________		Yes	No	________
________		Yes	No	________
________		Yes	No	________

TUESDAY: | | **Need it?** | | **AMOUNT**

________		Yes	No	________
________		Yes	No	________
________		Yes	No	________
________		Yes	No	________
________		Yes	No	________
________		Yes	No	________

WEDNESDAY: | | **Need it?** | | **AMOUNT**

________		Yes	No	________
________		Yes	No	________
________		Yes	No	________
________		Yes	No	________
________		Yes	No	________
________		Yes	No	________

EXPENSES:

INCOME   1 SOURCE: 2 SOURCE: 3 SOURCE:

THURSDAY:

Need it?   AMOUNT

Yes	No
Yes	No
Yes	No
Yes	No
Yes	No
Yes	No

FRIDAY:

Need it?   AMOUNT

Yes	No
Yes	No
Yes	No
Yes	No
Yes	No
Yes	No

WEEKEND:

Need it?   AMOUNT

Yes	No
Yes	No
Yes	No
Yes	No
Yes	No
Yes	No

TOTAL WEEKLY EXPENSES:

INCOME   4 SOURCE: 5 SOURCE: 6 SOURCE:

weekly "where's my money" part

Monday:

Need it? | Amount

Yes / No
Yes / No
Yes / No
Yes / No
Yes / No
Yes / No

Tuesday:

Need it? | Amount

Yes / No
Yes / No
Yes / No
Yes / No
Yes / No
Yes / No

Wednesday:

Need it? | Amount

Yes / No
Yes / No
Yes / No
Yes / No
Yes / No
Yes / No

Expenses:

Income   1 source: 2 source: 3 source:

THURSDAY:

	Need it?	AMOUNT
_______________	Yes No	_______________
_______________	Yes No	
_______________	Yes No	_______________
_______________	Yes No	
_______________	Yes No	_______________
_______________	Yes No	_______________

FRIDAY:

	Need it?	AMOUNT
_______________	Yes No	_______________
_______________	Yes No	
_______________	Yes No	_______________
_______________	Yes No	
_______________	Yes No	_______________
_______________	Yes No	_______________

Weekend:

	Need it?	AMOUNT
_______________	Yes No	_______________
_______________	Yes No	
_______________	Yes No	_______________
_______________	Yes No	
_______________	Yes No	_______________
_______________	Yes No	_______________

TOTAL WEEKLY EXPENSES:

INCOME   4 SOURCE: 5 SOURCE: 6 SOURCE:

weekly "where's my money" part

MONDAY:

Need it? AMOUNT

Yes	No
Yes	No
Yes	No
Yes	No
Yes	No
Yes	No

TUESDAY:

Need it? AMOUNT

Yes	No
Yes	No
Yes	No
Yes	No
Yes	No
Yes	No

WEDNESDAY:

Need it? AMOUNT

Yes	No
Yes	No
Yes	No
Yes	No
Yes	No
Yes	No

EXPENSES:

INCOME   1 SOURCE: 2 SOURCE: 3 SOURCE:

Thursday:

Need it?   Amount

Yes No

Yes No

Yes No

Yes No

Yes No

Yes No

Friday:

Need it?   Amount

Yes No

Yes No

Yes No

Yes No

Yes No

Yes No

Weekend:

Need it?   Amount

Yes No

Yes No

Yes No

Yes No

Yes No

Yes No

Total weekly Expenses:

Income   4 Source: 5 Source: 6 Source:

WRITE SOME IMPORTANT NOTES HERE:

MONTHLY BUDGET WORKSHEET

MONTH: YEAR:

Starting
debt

MONTHLY INCOME
1 SOURCE:
2 SOURCE:

3 SOURCE: 5 SOURCE:
4 SOURCE:

TOTAL:

EXPENSES	SPENT
Rent/Mortgage	
Electric	
Water	
Phone/Cell	
Internet	
Health insurance	
Life insurance	
Car insurance	
Gas/Other transport	
Car payment	
Gifts/Books/Cosmetic	
Cloths	
Entertainment	
Eating out	
Groceries	
Utilities	
Pets	
Charity	
Unexpected	
Savings	
TOTAL:	

MONTHLY
INCOME

−

TOTAL
EXPENSES

=

Total left to apply
to debts

Debts	Applied amount	Still Owe
_____	_____	_____
_____	_____	_____
_____	_____	_____
_____	_____	_____
_____	_____	_____
_____	_____	_____
_____	_____	_____
_____	_____	_____
_____	_____	_____
_____	_____	_____

Total
debt:

weekly "where's my money" part

MONDAY:

Need it?　　AMOUNT

	Yes	No
	Yes	No
	Yes	No
	Yes	No
	Yes	No
	Yes	No

TUESDAY:

Need it?　　AMOUNT

	Yes	No
	Yes	No
	Yes	No
	Yes	No
	Yes	No
	Yes	No

WEDNESDAY:

Need it?　　AMOUNT

	Yes	No
	Yes	No
	Yes	No
	Yes	No
	Yes	No
	Yes	No

EXPENSES:

INCOME　　1 SOURCE:　　2 SOURCE:　　3 SOURCE:

THURSDAY:

	Need it?		AMOUNT
_______________	Yes	No	__________
_______________	Yes	No	__________
_______________	Yes	No	__________
_______________	Yes	No	__________
_______________	Yes	No	__________
_______________	Yes	No	__________

FRIDAY:

	Need it?		AMOUNT
_______________	Yes	No	__________
_______________	Yes	No	__________
_______________	Yes	No	__________
_______________	Yes	No	__________
_______________	Yes	No	__________
_______________	Yes	No	__________

Weekend:

	Need it?		AMOUNT
_______________	Yes	No	__________
_______________	Yes	No	__________
_______________	Yes	No	__________
_______________	Yes	No	__________
_______________	Yes	No	__________
_______________	Yes	No	__________

Total weekly Expenses:

INCOME   4 SOURCE: 5 SOURCE: 6 SOURCE:

weekly "where's my money" part

MONDAY:

	Need it?		AMOUNT
	Yes	No	
	Yes	No	
	Yes	No	
	Yes	No	
	Yes	No	
	Yes	No	

TUESDAY:

	Need it?		AMOUNT
	Yes	No	
	Yes	No	
	Yes	No	
	Yes	No	
	Yes	No	
	Yes	No	

WEDNESDAY:

	Need it?		AMOUNT
	Yes	No	
	Yes	No	
	Yes	No	
	Yes	No	
	Yes	No	
	Yes	No	

EXPENSES:

INCOME   1 SOURCE: 2 SOURCE: 3 SOURCE:

THURSDAY:

	Need it?	Amount
	Yes / No	
	Yes / No	
	Yes / No	
	Yes / No	
	Yes / No	
	Yes / No	

FRIDAY:

	Need it?	Amount
	Yes / No	
	Yes / No	
	Yes / No	
	Yes / No	
	Yes / No	
	Yes / No	

WEEKEND:

	Need it?	Amount
	Yes / No	
	Yes / No	
	Yes / No	
	Yes / No	
	Yes / No	
	Yes / No	

Total weekly Expenses:

INCOME 4 SOURCE: 5 SOURCE: 6 SOURCE:

weekly "where's my money" part

MONDAY:

	Need it?		AMOUNT
______________	Yes	No	__________
______________	Yes	No	__________
______________	Yes	No	__________
______________	Yes	No	__________
______________	Yes	No	__________
______________	Yes	No	__________

TUESDAY:

	Need it?		AMOUNT
______________	Yes	No	__________
______________	Yes	No	__________
______________	Yes	No	__________
______________	Yes	No	__________
______________	Yes	No	__________
______________	Yes	No	__________

WEDNESDAY:

	Need it?		AMOUNT
______________	Yes	No	__________
______________	Yes	No	__________
______________	Yes	No	__________
______________	Yes	No	__________
______________	Yes	No	__________
______________	Yes	No	__________

EXPENSES:

INCOME   1 SOURCE: 2 SOURCE: 3 SOURCE:

THURSDAY:

	Need it?	AMOUNT
____________________	Yes / No	____________
____________________	Yes / No	____________
____________________	Yes / No	____________
____________________	Yes / No	____________
____________________	Yes / No	____________
____________________	Yes / No	____________

FRIDAY:

	Need it?	AMOUNT
____________________	Yes / No	____________
____________________	Yes / No	____________
____________________	Yes / No	____________
____________________	Yes / No	____________
____________________	Yes / No	____________
____________________	Yes / No	____________

Weekend:

	Need it?	AMOUNT
____________________	Yes / No	____________
____________________	Yes / No	____________
____________________	Yes / No	____________
____________________	Yes / No	____________
____________________	Yes / No	____________
____________________	Yes / No	____________

Total weekly Expenses:

INCOME   4 SOURCE: 5 SOURCE: 6 SOURCE:

Weekly "Where's My Money" Part

MONDAY: Need it?   AMOUNT

Yes	No
Yes	No
Yes	No
Yes	No
Yes	No
Yes	No

____

____

____

____

TUESDAY: Need it?   AMOUNT

Yes	No
Yes	No
Yes	No
Yes	No
Yes	No
Yes	No

WEDNESDAY: Need it?   AMOUNT

Yes	No
Yes	No
Yes	No
Yes	No
Yes	No
Yes	No

EXPENSES:

INCOME   1 SOURCE: 2 SOURCE: 3 SOURCE:

THURSDAY: Need it?   AMOUNT

	Yes	No	
_____	Yes	No	_____
_____	Yes	No	_____
_____	Yes	No	_____
_____	Yes	No	_____
_____	Yes	No	_____
_____	Yes	No	_____

FRIDAY: Need it?   AMOUNT

	Yes	No	
_____	Yes	No	_____
_____	Yes	No	_____
_____	Yes	No	_____
_____	Yes	No	_____
_____	Yes	No	_____
_____	Yes	No	_____

Weekend: Need it?   AMOUNT

	Yes	No	
_____	Yes	No	_____
_____	Yes	No	_____
_____	Yes	No	_____
_____	Yes	No	_____
_____	Yes	No	_____
_____	Yes	No	_____

TOTAL weekly Expenses:

INCOME   4 SOURCE: 5 SOURCE: 6 SOURCE:

Weekly "where's my money" part

MONDAY:

	Need it?		AMOUNT
_______________________	Yes	No	_______
_______________________	Yes	No	_______
_______________________	Yes	No	_______
_______________________	Yes	No	_______
_______________________	Yes	No	_______
_______________________	Yes	No	_______

Tuesday:

	Need it?		AMOUNT
_______________________	Yes	No	_______
_______________________	Yes	No	_______
_______________________	Yes	No	_______
_______________________	Yes	No	_______
_______________________	Yes	No	_______
_______________________	Yes	No	_______

Wednesday:

	Need it?		AMOUNT
_______________________	Yes	No	_______
_______________________	Yes	No	_______
_______________________	Yes	No	_______
_______________________	Yes	No	_______
_______________________	Yes	No	_______
_______________________	Yes	No	_______

EXPENSES:

INCOME   1 SOURCE: 2 SOURCE: 3 SOURCE:

THURSDAY: Need it?   AMOUNT

____________________________   Yes   NO   ____________
____________________________   Yes   NO   ____________
____________________________   Yes   NO   ____________
____________________________   Yes   NO   ____________
____________________________   Yes   NO   ____________
____________________________   Yes   NO   ____________

FRIDAY: Need it?   AMOUNT

____________________________   Yes   NO   ____________
____________________________   Yes   NO   ____________
____________________________   Yes   NO   ____________
____________________________   Yes   NO   ____________
____________________________   Yes   NO   ____________
____________________________   Yes   NO   ____________

WEEKEND: Need it?   AMOUNT

____________________________   Yes   NO   ____________
____________________________   Yes   NO   ____________
____________________________   Yes   NO   ____________
____________________________   Yes   NO   ____________
____________________________   Yes   NO   ____________
____________________________   Yes   NO   ____________

TOTAL WEEKLY EXPENSES:

INCOME   4 SOURCE: 5 SOURCE: 6 SOURCE:

WRite some imPORtant Notes HeRe:

MONTHLY BUDGET WORKSHEET

MONTH: YEAR:

Starting
debt

MONTHLY INCOME
1 Source:
2 Source:

3 Source: 5 Source:
4 Source:

Total:

Expenses	Spent
Rent/Mortgage	
Electric	
Water	
Phone/Cell	
Internet	
Health insurance	
Life insurance	
Car insurance	
Gas/Other transport	
Car payment	
Gifts/Books/Cosmetic	
Cloths	
Entertainment	
Eating out	
Groceries	
Utilities	
Pets	
Charity	
Unexpected	
Savings	
Total:	

MONTHLY
INCOME

−

Total
expenses

=

Total left to apply
to debts

Debts	Applied amount	Still Owe
___	___	___
___	___	___
___	___	___
___	___	___
___	___	___
___	___	___
___	___	___
___	___	___
___	___	___
___	___	___
___	___	___

Total debt:

Weekly "Where's My Money" Part

Monday: Need it?   Amount

_______________________________   Yes No   _______________
_______________________________   Yes No   _______________
_______________________________   Yes No   _______________
_______________________________   Yes No   _______________
_______________________________   Yes No   _______________
_______________________________   Yes No   _______________

Tuesday: Need it?   Amount

_______________________________   Yes No   _______________
_______________________________   Yes No   _______________
_______________________________   Yes No   _______________
_______________________________   Yes No   _______________
_______________________________   Yes No   _______________
_______________________________   Yes No   _______________

Wednesday: Need it?   Amount

_______________________________   Yes No   _______________
_______________________________   Yes No   _______________
_______________________________   Yes No   _______________
_______________________________   Yes No   _______________
_______________________________   Yes No   _______________
_______________________________   Yes No   _______________

Expenses:

Income   1 Source: 2 Source: 3 Source:

THURSDAY:

	Need it?		AMOUNT
	Yes	No	
	Yes	No	
	Yes	No	
	Yes	No	
	Yes	No	
	Yes	No	

FRIDAY:

	Need it?		AMOUNT
	Yes	No	
	Yes	No	
	Yes	No	
	Yes	No	
	Yes	No	
	Yes	No	

Weekend:

	Need it?		AMOUNT
	Yes	No	
	Yes	No	
	Yes	No	
	Yes	No	
	Yes	No	
	Yes	No	

TOTAL WEEKLY EXPENSES:

INCOME   4 SOURCE: 5 SOURCE: 6 SOURCE:

weekly "where's my money" part

MONDAY:

	Need it?		AMOUNT
____________	Yes	No	______
____________	Yes	No	______
____________	Yes	No	______
____________	Yes	No	______
____________	Yes	No	______
____________	Yes	No	______

TUESDAY:

	Need it?		AMOUNT
____________	Yes	No	______
____________	Yes	No	______
____________	Yes	No	______
____________	Yes	No	______
____________	Yes	No	______
____________	Yes	No	______

WEDNESDAY:

	Need it?		AMOUNT
____________	Yes	No	______
____________	Yes	No	______
____________	Yes	No	______
____________	Yes	No	______
____________	Yes	No	______
____________	Yes	No	______

EXPENSES:

INCOME   1 SOURCE: 2 SOURCE: 3 SOURCE:

Thursday:

Need it?   Amount

Yes	No
Yes	No
Yes	No
Yes	No
Yes	No
Yes	No

Friday:

Need it?   Amount

Yes	No
Yes	No
Yes	No
Yes	No
Yes	No
Yes	No

Weekend:

Need it?   Amount

Yes	No
Yes	No
Yes	No
Yes	No
Yes	No
Yes	No

Total weekly Expenses:

Income   4 Source: 5 Source: 6 Source:

weekly "where's my money" part

MONDAY:

		Need it?		AMOUNT
_____________		Yes / No		_______
_____________		Yes / No		_______
_____________		Yes / No		_______
_____________		Yes / No		_______
_____________		Yes / No		_______
		Yes / No		

TUESDAY:

		Need it?		AMOUNT
_____________		Yes / No		_______
_____________		Yes / No		_______
_____________		Yes / No		_______
_____________		Yes / No		_______
_____________		Yes / No		_______
		Yes / No		

WEDNESDAY:

		Need it?		AMOUNT
_____________		Yes / No		_______
_____________		Yes / No		_______
_____________		Yes / No		_______
_____________		Yes / No		_______
_____________		Yes / No		_______
		Yes / No		

EXPENSES:

INCOME   1 SOURCE: 2 SOURCE: 3 SOURCE:

THURSDAY:

	Need it?		AMOUNT
_______	Yes	No	_______
_______	Yes	No	_______
_______	Yes	No	_______
_______	Yes	No	_______
_______	Yes	No	_______
_______	Yes	No	_______

FRIDAY:

	Need it?		AMOUNT
_______	Yes	No	_______
_______	Yes	No	_______
_______	Yes	No	_______
_______	Yes	No	_______
_______	Yes	No	_______
_______	Yes	No	_______

Weekend:

	Need it?		AMOUNT
_______	Yes	No	_______
_______	Yes	No	_______
_______	Yes	No	_______
_______	Yes	No	_______
_______	Yes	No	_______
_______	Yes	No	_______

Total weekly Expenses:

INCOME   4 SOURCE: 5 SOURCE: 6 SOURCE:

Weekly "Where's My Money" Part

MONDAY: Need it?   AMOUNT

Yes	No
Yes	No
Yes	No
Yes	No
Yes	No
Yes	No

TUESDAY: Need it?   AMOUNT

Yes	No
Yes	No
Yes	No
Yes	No
Yes	No
Yes	No

WEDNESDAY: Need it?   AMOUNT

Yes	No
Yes	No
Yes	No
Yes	No
Yes	No
Yes	No

EXPENSES:

INCOME   1 SOURCE: 2 SOURCE: 3 SOURCE:

THURSDAY: Need it?   AMOUNT

	Yes	No	
	Yes	No	
	Yes	No	
	Yes	No	
	Yes	No	
	Yes	No	

FRIDAY: Need it?   AMOUNT

	Yes	No	
	Yes	No	
	Yes	No	
	Yes	No	
	Yes	No	
	Yes	No	

WEEKEND: Need it?   AMOUNT

	Yes	No	
	Yes	No	
	Yes	No	
	Yes	No	
	Yes	No	
	Yes	No	

TOTAL WEEKLY EXPENSES:

INCOME   4 SOURCE: 5 SOURCE: 6 SOURCE:

Weekly "Where's My Money" Part

Monday: Need it?   Amount

_______________________________   [Yes] [No]   _______________
_______________________________   [Yes] [No]   _______________
_______________________________   [Yes] [No]   _______________
_______________________________   [Yes] [No]   _______________
_______________________________   [Yes] [No]   _______________
_______________________________   [Yes] [No]   _______________

Tuesday: Need it?   Amount

_______________________________   [Yes] [No]   _______________
_______________________________   [Yes] [No]   _______________
_______________________________   [Yes] [No]   _______________
_______________________________   [Yes] [No]   _______________
_______________________________   [Yes] [No]   _______________
_______________________________   [Yes] [No]   _______________

Wednesday: Need it?   Amount

_______________________________   [Yes] [No]   _______________
_______________________________   [Yes] [No]   _______________
_______________________________   [Yes] [No]   _______________
_______________________________   [Yes] [No]   _______________
_______________________________   [Yes] [No]   _______________
_______________________________   [Yes] [No]   _______________

Expenses:

Income   1 Source: 2 Source: 3 Source:

Thursday: Need it?   Amount

Yes	No	
Yes	No	
Yes	No	
Yes	No	
Yes	No	
Yes	No	

Friday: Need it?   Amount

Yes	No	
Yes	No	
Yes	No	
Yes	No	
Yes	No	
Yes	No	

Weekend: Need it?   Amount

Yes	No	
Yes	No	
Yes	No	
Yes	No	
Yes	No	
Yes	No	

Total weekly Expenses:

Income   4 Source: 5 Source: 6 Source:

WRite some important Notes Here:

MONTHLY BUDGET WORKSHEET

MONTH: YEAR:

Starting Debt

MONTHLY INCOME
1 SOURCE:
2 SOURCE:

3 SOURCE: 5 SOURCE:
4 SOURCE:

TOTAL:

Expenses	Spent
Rent/Mortgage	
Electric	
Water	
Phone/Cell	
Internet	
Health insurance	
Life insurance	
Car insurance	
Gas/Other transport	
Car payment	
Gifts/Books/Cosmetic	
Cloths	
Entertainment	
Eating out	
Groceries	
Utilities	
Pets	
Charity	
Unexpected	
Savings	
TOTAL:	

MONTHLY INCOME

−

TOTAL expenses

=

Total left to apply to debts

Debts	Applied amount	Still Owe
___	___	___
___	___	___
___	___	___
___	___	___
___	___	___
___	___	___
___	___	___
___	___	___
___	___	___
___	___	___
___	___	___

Total Debt:

Weekly "Where's My Money" Part

Monday:

	Need it?		Amount
_______________________	Yes	No	__________
_______________________	Yes	No	__________
_______________________	Yes	No	__________
_______________________	Yes	No	__________
_______________________	Yes	No	__________
_______________________	Yes	No	__________

Tuesday:

	Need it?		Amount
_______________________	Yes	No	__________
_______________________	Yes	No	__________
_______________________	Yes	No	__________
_______________________	Yes	No	__________
_______________________	Yes	No	__________
_______________________	Yes	No	__________

Wednesday:

	Need it?		Amount
_______________________	Yes	No	__________
_______________________	Yes	No	__________
_______________________	Yes	No	__________
_______________________	Yes	No	__________
_______________________	Yes	No	__________
_______________________	Yes	No	__________

Expenses:

Income   1 Source: 2 Source: 3 Source:

THURSDAY:

	Need it?		AMOUNT
____________	Yes	No	________
____________	Yes	No	________
____________	Yes	No	________
____________	Yes	No	________
____________	Yes	No	________
____________	Yes	No	

FRIDAY:

	Need it?		AMOUNT
____________	Yes	No	________
____________	Yes	No	________
____________	Yes	No	________
____________	Yes	No	________
____________	Yes	No	________
____________	Yes	No	

Weekend:

	Need it?		AMOUNT
____________	Yes	No	________
____________	Yes	No	________
____________	Yes	No	________
____________	Yes	No	________
____________	Yes	No	________
____________	Yes	No	

TOTAL weekly Expenses:

INCOME   4 SOURCe: 5 SOURCe: 6 SOURCe:

weekly "where's my money" part

MONDAY:

	Need it?	AMOUNT
_______________	Yes / No	__________
_______________	Yes / No	__________
_______________	Yes / No	__________
_______________	Yes / No	__________
_______________	Yes / No	__________
_______________	Yes / No	__________

TUESDAY:

	Need it?	AMOUNT
_______________	Yes / No	__________
_______________	Yes / No	__________
_______________	Yes / No	__________
_______________	Yes / No	__________
_______________	Yes / No	__________
_______________	Yes / No	__________

Wednesday:

	Need it?	AMOUNT
_______________	Yes / No	__________
_______________	Yes / No	__________
_______________	Yes / No	__________
_______________	Yes / No	__________
_______________	Yes / No	__________
_______________	Yes / No	__________

EXPENSES:

INCOME   1 SOURCE: 2 SOURCE: 3 SOURCE:

Thursday:

	Need it?	Amount
____________________	Yes No	__________
____________________	Yes No	__________
____________________	Yes No	__________
____________________	Yes No	__________
____________________	Yes No	__________
____________________	Yes No	__________

Friday:

	Need it?	Amount
____________________	Yes No	__________
____________________	Yes No	__________
____________________	Yes No	__________
____________________	Yes No	__________
____________________	Yes No	__________
____________________	Yes No	__________

Weekend:

	Need it?	Amount
____________________	Yes No	__________
____________________	Yes No	__________
____________________	Yes No	__________
____________________	Yes No	__________
____________________	Yes No	__________
____________________	Yes No	__________

Total weekly Expenses:

Income   4 Source: 5 Source: 6 Source:

weekly "where's my money" part

MONDAY:

	Need it?		AMOUNT
__________________	Yes	No	__________
__________________	Yes	No	__________
__________________	Yes	No	__________
__________________	Yes	No	__________
__________________	Yes	No	__________
__________________	Yes	No	__________

TUESDAY:

	Need it?		AMOUNT
__________________	Yes	No	__________
__________________	Yes	No	__________
__________________	Yes	No	__________
__________________	Yes	No	__________
__________________	Yes	No	__________
__________________	Yes	No	__________

WEDNESDAY:

	Need it?		AMOUNT
__________________	Yes	No	__________
__________________	Yes	No	__________
__________________	Yes	No	__________
__________________	Yes	No	__________
__________________	Yes	No	__________
__________________	Yes	No	__________

EXPENSES:

INCOME   1 SOURCE: 2 SOURCE: 3 SOURCE:

Thursday:

Need it?   Amount

Yes No
Yes No
Yes No
Yes No
Yes No
Yes No

Friday:

Need it?   Amount

Yes No
Yes No
Yes No
Yes No
Yes No
Yes No

Weekend:

Need it?   Amount

Yes No
Yes No
Yes No
Yes No
Yes No
Yes No

Total weekly Expenses:

Income   4 Source: 5 Source: 6 Source:

weekly "where's my money" part

Monday:

	Need it?		Amount
	Yes	No	
	Yes	No	
	Yes	No	
	Yes	No	
	Yes	No	
	Yes	No	

Tuesday:

	Need it?		Amount
	Yes	No	
	Yes	No	
	Yes	No	
	Yes	No	
	Yes	No	
	Yes	No	

Wednesday:

	Need it?		Amount
	Yes	No	
	Yes	No	
	Yes	No	
	Yes	No	
	Yes	No	
	Yes	No	

Expenses:

Income   1 Source: 2 Source: 3 Source:

THURSDAY:

	Need it?	Amount
	Yes No	
	Yes No	
	Yes No	
	Yes No	
	Yes No	
	Yes No	

FRIDAY:

	Need it?	Amount
	Yes No	
	Yes No	
	Yes No	
	Yes No	
	Yes No	
	Yes No	

WEEKEND:

	Need it?	Amount
	Yes No	
	Yes No	
	Yes No	
	Yes No	
	Yes No	
	Yes No	

Total weekly Expenses:

INCOME   4 SOURCE: 5 SOURCE: 6 SOURCE:

weekly "where's my money" part

MONDAY:

	Need it?		AMOUNT
______________________	Yes	No	__________
______________________	Yes	No	__________
______________________	Yes	No	__________
______________________	Yes	No	__________
______________________	Yes	No	__________
______________________	Yes	No	__________

Tuesday:

	Need it?		AMOUNT
______________________	Yes	No	__________
______________________	Yes	No	__________
______________________	Yes	No	__________
______________________	Yes	No	__________
______________________	Yes	No	__________
______________________	Yes	No	__________

Wednesday:

	Need it?		AMOUNT
______________________	Yes	No	__________
______________________	Yes	No	__________
______________________	Yes	No	__________
______________________	Yes	No	__________
______________________	Yes	No	__________
______________________	Yes	No	__________

EXPENSES:

INCOME   1 SOURCE: 2 SOURCE: 3 SOURCE:

Thursday:

	Need it?	Amount
___________________	Yes No	_________
___________________	Yes No	_________
___________________	Yes No	_________
___________________	Yes No	_________
___________________	Yes No	_________
___________________	Yes No	_________

Friday:

	Need it?	Amount
___________________	Yes No	_________
___________________	Yes No	_________
___________________	Yes No	_________
___________________	Yes No	_________
___________________	Yes No	_________
___________________	Yes No	_________

Weekend:

	Need it?	Amount
___________________	Yes No	_________
___________________	Yes No	_________
___________________	Yes No	_________
___________________	Yes No	_________
___________________	Yes No	_________
___________________	Yes No	_________

Total weekly Expenses:

Income   4 Source: 5 Source: 6 Source:

Write some important Notes here:

MONTHLY BUDGET WORKSHEET

MONTH: YEAR:

Starting Debt

MONTHLY INCOME
1 SOURCE:
2 SOURCE:
3 SOURCE:
4 SOURCE:
5 SOURCE:
Total:

Expenses	Spent
Rent/Mortgage	
Electric	
Water	
Phone/Cell	
Internet	
Health insurance	
Life insurance	
Car insurance	
Gas/Other transport	
Car payment	
Gifts/Books/Cosmetic	
Cloths	
Entertainment	
Eating out	
Groceries	
Utilities	
Pets	
Charity	
Unexpected	
Savings	
TOTAL:	

MONTHLY INCOME

-

Total expenses

=

Total left to apply to debts

Debts	Applied Amount	Still Owe

Total Debt:

weekly "where's my money" part

MONDAY: Need it?   AMOUNT

	Yes	No	
	Yes	No	
	Yes	No	
	Yes	No	
	Yes	No	
	Yes	No	

TUESDAY: Need it?   AMOUNT

	Yes	No	
	Yes	No	
	Yes	No	
	Yes	No	
	Yes	No	
	Yes	No	

WEDNESDAY: Need it?   AMOUNT

	Yes	No	
	Yes	No	
	Yes	No	
	Yes	No	
	Yes	No	
	Yes	No	

EXPENSES:

INCOME   1 SOURCE: 2 SOURCE: 3 SOURCE:

<table>
<tr><td></td><td>Week:</td><td>Month:</td><td>Year:</td></tr>
</table>

Thursday:

	Need it?		Amount
	Yes	No	
	Yes	No	
	Yes	No	
	Yes	No	
	Yes	No	
	Yes	No	

Friday:

	Need it?		Amount
	Yes	No	
	Yes	No	
	Yes	No	
	Yes	No	
	Yes	No	
	Yes	No	

Weekend:

	Need it?		Amount
	Yes	No	
	Yes	No	
	Yes	No	
	Yes	No	
	Yes	No	
	Yes	No	

Total weekly Expenses:

Income   4 Source: 5 Source: 6 Source:

Weekly "Where's My Money" Part

MONDAY: Need it?   AMOUNT

Yes	No
Yes	No
Yes	No
Yes	No
Yes	No
Yes	No

TUESDAY: Need it?   AMOUNT

Yes	No
Yes	No
Yes	No
Yes	No
Yes	No
Yes	No

WEDNESDAY: Need it?   AMOUNT

Yes	No
Yes	No
Yes	No
Yes	No
Yes	No
Yes	No

EXPENSES:

INCOME   1 SOURCE: 2 SOURCE: 3 SOURCE:

THURSDAY:

Need it? Amount

Yes No
Yes No
Yes No
Yes No
Yes No
Yes No

FRIDAY:

Need it? Amount

Yes No
Yes No
Yes No
Yes No
Yes No
Yes No

WEEKEND:

Need it? Amount

Yes No
Yes No
Yes No
Yes No
Yes No
Yes No

TOTAL weekly EXPENSES:

INCOME   4 SOURCE: 5 SOURCE: 6 SOURCE:

Weekly "Where's My Money" Part

MONDAY:

	Need it?		AMOUNT
____________________	Yes	No	__________
____________________	Yes	No	__________
____________________	Yes	No	__________
____________________	Yes	No	__________
____________________	Yes	No	__________
____________________	Yes	No	

TUESDAY:

	Need it?		AMOUNT
____________________	Yes	No	__________
____________________	Yes	No	__________
____________________	Yes	No	__________
____________________	Yes	No	__________
____________________	Yes	No	__________
____________________	Yes	No	

WEDNESDAY:

	Need it?		AMOUNT
____________________	Yes	No	__________
____________________	Yes	No	__________
____________________	Yes	No	__________
____________________	Yes	No	__________
____________________	Yes	No	__________
____________________	Yes	No	__________

EXPENSES:

INCOME   1 SOURCE: 2 SOURCE: 3 SOURCE:

THURSDAY:

Need it?   AMOUNT

- Yes / No
- Yes / No
- Yes / No
- Yes / No
- Yes / No
- Yes / No

FRIDAY:

Need it?   AMOUNT

- Yes / No
- Yes / No
- Yes / No
- Yes / No
- Yes / No
- Yes / No

Weekend:

Need it?   AMOUNT

- Yes / No
- Yes / No
- Yes / No
- Yes / No
- Yes / No
- Yes / No

TOTAL weekly EXPENSES:

INCOME   4 SOURCE: 5 SOURCE: 6 SOURCE:

weekly "where's my money" Part

MONDAY:

	Need it?		AMOUNT
______________	Yes	NO	__________
______________	Yes	NO	__________
______________	Yes	NO	__________
______________	Yes	NO	__________
______________	Yes	NO	__________
______________	Yes	NO	__________

TUESDAY:

	Need it?		AMOUNT
______________	Yes	NO	__________
______________	Yes	NO	__________
______________	Yes	NO	__________
______________	Yes	NO	__________
______________	Yes	NO	__________
______________	Yes	NO	__________

WEDNESDAY:

	Need it?		AMOUNT
______________	Yes	NO	__________
______________	Yes	NO	__________
______________	Yes	NO	__________
______________	Yes	NO	__________
______________	Yes	NO	__________
______________	Yes	NO	__________

EXPENSES:

INCOME   1 SOURCE: 2 SOURCE: 3 SOURCE:

THURSDAY:

Need it?		AMOUNT
Yes	No	
Yes	No	
Yes	No	
Yes	No	
Yes	No	
Yes	No	

FRIDAY:

Need it?		AMOUNT
Yes	No	
Yes	No	
Yes	No	
Yes	No	
Yes	No	
Yes	No	

WEEKEND:

Need it?		AMOUNT
Yes	No	
Yes	No	
Yes	No	
Yes	No	
Yes	No	
Yes	No	

TOTAL WEEKLY EXPENSES:

INCOME   4 SOURCE: 5 SOURCE: 6 SOURCE:

weekly "where's my money" part

MONDAY:

	Need it?	Amount
__________________	Yes No	__________
__________________	Yes No	__________
__________________	Yes No	__________
__________________	Yes No	__________
__________________	Yes No	__________
__________________	Yes No	__________

Tuesday:

	Need it?	Amount
__________________	Yes No	__________
__________________	Yes No	__________
__________________	Yes No	__________
__________________	Yes No	__________
__________________	Yes No	__________
__________________	Yes No	__________

Wednesday:

	Need it?	Amount
__________________	Yes No	__________
__________________	Yes No	__________
__________________	Yes No	__________
__________________	Yes No	__________
__________________	Yes No	__________
__________________	Yes No	__________

EXPenses:

INCOME   1 SOURCE: 2 SOURCE: 3 SOURCE:

THURSDAY: Need it?   AMOUNT

_______________________________   Yes   No   _______________
_______________________________   Yes   No   _______________
_______________________________   Yes   No   _______________
_______________________________   Yes   No   _______________
_______________________________   Yes   No   _______________
_______________________________   Yes   No   _______________

FRIDAY: Need it?   AMOUNT

_______________________________   Yes   No   _______________
_______________________________   Yes   No   _______________
_______________________________   Yes   No   _______________
_______________________________   Yes   No   _______________
_______________________________   Yes   No   _______________
_______________________________   Yes   No   _______________

Weekend: Need it?   AMOUNT

_______________________________   Yes   No   _______________
_______________________________   Yes   No   _______________
_______________________________   Yes   No   _______________
_______________________________   Yes   No   _______________
_______________________________   Yes   No   _______________
_______________________________   Yes   No   _______________

Total weekly Expenses:

INCOME   4 SOURCE: 5 SOURCE: 6 SOURCE:

WRite some imPoRtant Notes HeRe:

MONTHLY BUDGET WORKSHEET

MONTH: YEAR:

Starting
debt

MONTHLY INCOME
1 SOURCE:
2 SOURCE:

3 SOURCE: 5 SOURCE:
4 SOURCE:

Total:

Expenses	Spent
Rent/Mortgage	
Electric	
Water	
Phone/Cell	
Internet	
Health insurance	
Life insurance	
Car insurance	
Gas/other transport	
Car payment	
Gifts/Books/Cosmetic	
Cloths	
Entertainment	
Eating out	
Groceries	
Utilities	
Pets	
Charity	
Unexpected	
Savings	
TOTAL:	

MONTHLY
INCOME

-

Total
expenses

=

Total left to apply
to debts

Debts	Applied amount	Still owe
___	___	___
___	___	___
___	___	___
___	___	___
___	___	___
___	___	___
___	___	___
___	___	___
___	___	___

Total
debt:

Weekly "Where's my money" part

MONDAY:

		Need it?		AMOUNT
____________		Yes	No	____________
____________		Yes	No	____________
____________		Yes	No	____________
____________		Yes	No	____________
____________		Yes	No	____________
____________		Yes	No	____________

TUESDAY:

		Need it?		AMOUNT
____________		Yes	No	____________
____________		Yes	No	____________
____________		Yes	No	____________
____________		Yes	No	____________
____________		Yes	No	____________
____________		Yes	No	____________

WEDNESDAY:

		Need it?		AMOUNT
____________		Yes	No	____________
____________		Yes	No	____________
____________		Yes	No	____________
____________		Yes	No	____________
____________		Yes	No	____________
____________		Yes	No	____________

EXPENSES:

INCOME   1 SOURCE: 2 SOURCE: 3 SOURCE:

Week: MONTH: YEAR:

THURSDAY:

	Need it?		AMOUNT
	Yes	No	
	Yes	No	
	Yes	No	
	Yes	No	
	Yes	No	
	Yes	No	

FRIDAY:

	Need it?		AMOUNT
	Yes	No	
	Yes	No	
	Yes	No	
	Yes	No	
	Yes	No	
	Yes	No	

WEEKEND:

	Need it?		AMOUNT
	Yes	No	
	Yes	No	
	Yes	No	
	Yes	No	
	Yes	No	
	Yes	No	

TOTAL WEEKLY EXPENSES:

INCOME   4 SOURCE: 5 SOURCE: 6 SOURCE:

weekly "where's my money" part

MONDAY:

		Need it?		AMOUNT
	Yes	No		
	Yes	No		
	Yes	No		
	Yes	No		
	Yes	No		
	Yes	No		

TUESDAY:

		Need it?		AMOUNT
	Yes	No		
	Yes	No		
	Yes	No		
	Yes	No		
	Yes	No		
	Yes	No		

WEDNESDAY:

		Need it?		AMOUNT
	Yes	No		
	Yes	No		
	Yes	No		
	Yes	No		
	Yes	No		
	Yes	No		

EXPENSES:

INCOME   1 SOURCE: 2 SOURCE: 3 SOURCE:

THURSDAY:

Need it?   AMOUNT

Yes	No
Yes	No
Yes	No
Yes	No
Yes	No
Yes	No

FRIDAY:

Need it?   AMOUNT

Yes	No
Yes	No
Yes	No
Yes	No
Yes	No
Yes	No

WEEKEND:

Need it?   AMOUNT

Yes	No
Yes	No
Yes	No
Yes	No
Yes	No
Yes	No

Total weekly Expenses:

INCOME   4 SOURCE: 5 SOURCE: 6 SOURCE:

Weekly "Where's My Money" Part

MONDAY: Need it?   AMOUNT

Yes	No	
Yes	No	
Yes	No	
Yes	No	
Yes	No	
Yes	No	

TUESDAY: Need it?   AMOUNT

Yes	No	
Yes	No	
Yes	No	
Yes	No	
Yes	No	
Yes	No	

WEDNESDAY: Need it?   AMOUNT

Yes	No	
Yes	No	
Yes	No	
Yes	No	
Yes	No	
Yes	No	

EXPENSES:

INCOME   1 SOURCE: 2 SOURCE: 3 SOURCE:

THURSDAY:

	Need it?		AMOUNT
__________	Yes	No	__________
__________	Yes	No	__________
__________	Yes	No	__________
__________	Yes	No	__________
__________	Yes	No	__________
__________	Yes	No	__________

FRIDAY:

	Need it?		AMOUNT
__________	Yes	No	__________
__________	Yes	No	__________
__________	Yes	No	__________
__________	Yes	No	__________
__________	Yes	No	__________
__________	Yes	No	__________

WeekenD:

	Need it?		AMOUNT
__________	Yes	No	__________
__________	Yes	No	__________
__________	Yes	No	__________
__________	Yes	No	__________
__________	Yes	No	__________
__________	Yes	No	__________

Total weekly Expenses:

INCOME   4 SOURCe: 5 SOURCe: 6 SOURCe:

weekly "where's my money" part

MONDAY:

	Need it?		AMOUNT

Yes / No
Yes / No
Yes / No
Yes / No
Yes / No
Yes / No

TUESDAY:

Need it?   AMOUNT

Yes / No
Yes / No
Yes / No
Yes / No
Yes / No
Yes / No

WEDNESDAY:

Need it?   AMOUNT

Yes / No
Yes / No
Yes / No
Yes / No
Yes / No
Yes / No

EXPENSES:

INCOME   1 SOURCE: 2 SOURCE: 3 SOURCE:

THURSDAY:

Need it?   AMOUNT

Yes   No
Yes   No
Yes   No
Yes   No
Yes   No
Yes   No

FRIDAY:

Need it?   AMOUNT

Yes   No
Yes   No
Yes   No
Yes   No
Yes   No
Yes   No

WEEKEND:

Need it?   AMOUNT

Yes   No
Yes   No
Yes   No
Yes   No
Yes   No
Yes   No

TOTAL WEEKLY EXPENSES:

INCOME   4 SOURCE: 5 SOURCE: 6 SOURCE:

Weekly "Where's My Money" Part

MONDAY:

	Need it?		AMOUNT
_______________	Yes	No	_______
_______________	Yes	No	_______
_______________	Yes	No	_______
_______________	Yes	No	_______
_______________	Yes	No	_______
_______________	Yes	No	_______

TUESDAY:

	Need it?		AMOUNT
_______________	Yes	No	_______
_______________	Yes	No	_______
_______________	Yes	No	_______
_______________	Yes	No	_______
_______________	Yes	No	_______
_______________	Yes	No	_______

WEDNESDAY:

	Need it?		AMOUNT
_______________	Yes	No	_______
_______________	Yes	No	_______
_______________	Yes	No	_______
_______________	Yes	No	_______
_______________	Yes	No	_______
_______________	Yes	No	_______

EXPENSES:

INCOME   1 SOURCE: 2 SOURCE: 3 SOURCE:

<table>
<tr><td>Week:</td><td>Month:</td><td>Year:</td></tr>
</table>

Thursday:

	Need it?	Amount
______________	Yes No	__________
______________	Yes No	__________
______________	Yes No	__________
______________	Yes No	__________
______________	Yes No	__________
______________	Yes No	__________

Friday:

	Need it?	Amount
______________	Yes No	__________
______________	Yes No	__________
______________	Yes No	__________
______________	Yes No	__________
______________	Yes No	__________
______________	Yes No	__________

Weekend:

	Need it?	Amount
______________	Yes No	__________
______________	Yes No	__________
______________	Yes No	__________
______________	Yes No	__________
______________	Yes No	__________
______________	Yes No	__________

Total weekly Expenses:

Income   4 Source: 5 Source: 6 Source:

Write some important Notes here:

MONTHLY BUDGET WORKSHEET

MONTH: YEAR:

STARTING DEBT

MONTHLY INCOME
1 SOURCE:
2 SOURCE:
3 SOURCE:
4 SOURCE:
5 SOURCE:
TOTAL:

EXPENSES	SPENT
Rent/Mortgage	
Electric	
Water	
Phone/Cell	
Internet	
Health insurance	
Life insurance	
Car insurance	
Gas/Other transport	
Car payment	
Gifts/Books/Cosmetic	
Cloths	
Entertainment	
Eating out	
Groceries	
Utilities	
Pets	
Charity	
Unexpected	
Savings	
TOTAL:	

MONTHLY INCOME

\-

TOTAL EXPENSES

=

TOTAL left to apply to debts

Debts	Applied amount	Still owe
___	___	___
___	___	___
___	___	___
___	___	___
___	___	___
___	___	___
___	___	___
___	___	___
___	___	___
___	___	___
___	___	___
___	___	___

TOTAL DEBT:

Weekly "Where's My Money" Part

MONDAY:

	Need it?	AMOUNT
_____________	Yes / No	_____________
_____________	Yes / No	_____________
_____________	Yes / No	_____________
_____________	Yes / No	_____________
_____________	Yes / No	_____________
_____________	Yes / No	_____________

TUESDAY:

	Need it?	AMOUNT
_____________	Yes / No	_____________
_____________	Yes / No	_____________
_____________	Yes / No	_____________
_____________	Yes / No	_____________
_____________	Yes / No	_____________
_____________	Yes / No	_____________

WEDNESDAY:

	Need it?	AMOUNT
_____________	Yes / No	_____________
_____________	Yes / No	_____________
_____________	Yes / No	_____________
_____________	Yes / No	_____________
_____________	Yes / No	_____________
_____________	Yes / No	_____________

EXPENSES:

INCOME   1 SOURCE: 2 SOURCE: 3 SOURCE:

Week: MONTH: YEAR:

THURSDAY:

Need it?   AMOUNT

Yes No
Yes No
Yes No
Yes No
Yes No
Yes No

FRIDAY:

Need it?   AMOUNT

Yes No
Yes No
Yes No
Yes No
Yes No
Yes No

Weekend:

Need it?   AMOUNT

Yes No
Yes No
Yes No
Yes No
Yes No
Yes No

Total weekly Expenses:

INCOME   4 SOURCE: 5 SOURCE: 6 SOURCE:

weekly "where's my money" Part

MONDAY:

	Need it?		AMOUNT
______________________	Yes	No	__________
______________________	Yes	No	__________
______________________	Yes	No	__________
______________________	Yes	No	__________
______________________	Yes	No	__________
______________________	Yes	No	__________

TUESDAY:

	Need it?		AMOUNT
______________________	Yes	No	__________
______________________	Yes	No	__________
______________________	Yes	No	__________
______________________	Yes	No	__________
______________________	Yes	No	__________
______________________	Yes	No	__________

WEDNESDAY:

	Need it?		AMOUNT
______________________	Yes	No	__________
______________________	Yes	No	__________
______________________	Yes	No	__________
______________________	Yes	No	__________
______________________	Yes	No	__________
______________________	Yes	No	__________

EXPENSES:

INCOME   1 SOURCE: 2 SOURCE: 3 SOURCE:

THURSDAY:

	Need it?		AMOUNT
____________________	Yes	No	__________
____________________	Yes	No	__________
____________________	Yes	No	__________
____________________	Yes	No	__________
____________________	Yes	No	__________
____________________	Yes	No	__________

FRIDAY:

	Need it?		AMOUNT
____________________	Yes	No	__________
____________________	Yes	No	__________
____________________	Yes	No	__________
____________________	Yes	No	__________
____________________	Yes	No	__________
____________________	Yes	No	__________

WEEKEND:

	Need it?		AMOUNT
____________________	Yes	No	__________
____________________	Yes	No	__________
____________________	Yes	No	__________
____________________	Yes	No	__________
____________________	Yes	No	__________
____________________	Yes	No	__________

TOTAL WEEKLY EXPENSES:

INCOME   4 SOURCE: 5 SOURCE: 6 SOURCE:

Weekly "Where's My Money" Part

MONDAY:

Need it?   AMOUNT

Yes	No	
Yes	No	
Yes	No	
Yes	No	
Yes	No	
Yes	No	

TUESDAY:

Need it?   AMOUNT

Yes	No	
Yes	No	
Yes	No	
Yes	No	
Yes	No	
Yes	No	

WEDNESDAY:

Need it?   AMOUNT

Yes	No	
Yes	No	
Yes	No	
Yes	No	
Yes	No	
Yes	No	

EXPENSES:

INCOME   1 SOURCE: 2 SOURCE: 3 SOURCE:

THURSDAY:

Need it?   AMOUNT

Yes   No
Yes   No
Yes   No
Yes   No
Yes   No
Yes   No

FRIDAY:

Need it?   AMOUNT

Yes   No
Yes   No
Yes   No
Yes   No
Yes   No
Yes   No

WEEKEND:

Need it?   AMOUNT

Yes   No
Yes   No
Yes   No
Yes   No
Yes   No
Yes   No

TOTAL WEEKLY EXPENSES:

INCOME   4 SOURCE: 5 SOURCE: 6 SOURCE:

weekly "where's my money" part

MONDAY:

	Need it?	AMOUNT
	Yes / No	
	Yes / No	
	Yes / No	
	Yes / No	
	Yes / No	
	Yes / No	

TUESDAY:

	Need it?	AMOUNT
	Yes / No	
	Yes / No	
	Yes / No	
	Yes / No	
	Yes / No	
	Yes / No	

WEDNESDAY:

	Need it?	AMOUNT
	Yes / No	
	Yes / No	
	Yes / No	
	Yes / No	
	Yes / No	
	Yes / No	

EXPENSES:

INCOME   1 SOURCE: 2 SOURCE: 3 SOURCE:

THURSDAY:

Need it?   AMOUNT

Yes	No
Yes	No
Yes	No
Yes	No
Yes	No
Yes	No

FRIDAY:

Need it?   AMOUNT

Yes	No
Yes	No
Yes	No
Yes	No
Yes	No
Yes	No

WEEKEND:

Need it?   AMOUNT

Yes	No
Yes	No
Yes	No
Yes	No
Yes	No
Yes	No

TOTAL WEEKLY EXPENSES:

INCOME   4 SOURCE: 5 SOURCE: 6 SOURCE:

weekly "where's my money" part

MONDAY:

	Need it?	AMOUNT
_______________________	Yes No	_____________
_______________________	Yes No	_____________
_______________________	Yes No	_____________
_______________________	Yes No	_____________
_______________________	Yes No	_____________
_______________________	Yes No	_____________

TUESDAY:

	Need it?	AMOUNT
_______________________	Yes No	_____________
_______________________	Yes No	_____________
_______________________	Yes No	_____________
_______________________	Yes No	_____________
_______________________	Yes No	_____________
_______________________	Yes No	_____________

WEDNESDAY:

	Need it?	AMOUNT
_______________________	Yes No	_____________
_______________________	Yes No	_____________
_______________________	Yes No	_____________
_______________________	Yes No	_____________
_______________________	Yes No	_____________
_______________________	Yes No	_____________

EXPENSES:

INCOME   1 SOURCE: 2 SOURCE: 3 SOURCE:

THURSDAY:

	Need it?		AMOUNT
________________	Yes	No	
________________	Yes	No	________
________________	Yes	No	________
________________	Yes	No	________
________________	Yes	No	________
________________	Yes	No	________

FRIDAY:

	Need it?		AMOUNT
________________	Yes	No	
________________	Yes	No	________
________________	Yes	No	________
________________	Yes	No	________
________________	Yes	No	________
________________	Yes	No	________

WEEKEND:

	Need it?		AMOUNT
________________	Yes	No	
________________	Yes	No	________
________________	Yes	No	________
________________	Yes	No	________
________________	Yes	No	________
________________	Yes	No	________

Total weekly Expenses:

INCOME   4 SOURCE: 5 SOURCE: 6 SOURCE:

Write some important Notes here:

MONTHLY BUDGET WORKSHEET

MONTH: YEAR:

Starting Debt

MONTHLY INCOME
1 SOURCE:
2 SOURCE:

3 SOURCE:
4 SOURCE:

5 SOURCE:

Total:

Expenses	Spent
Rent/Mortgage	
Electric	
Water	
Phone/Cell	
Internet	
Health insurance	
Life insurance	
Car insurance	
Gas/Other transport	
Car payment	
Gifts/Books/Cosmetic	
Cloths	
Entertainment	
Eating out	
Groceries	
Utilities	
Pets	
Charity	
Unexpected	
Savings	
TOTAL:	

MONTHLY INCOME

-

TOTAL EXPENSES

=

Total left to apply to debts

Debts	Applied amount	Still Owe
_____	_____	_____
_____	_____	_____
_____	_____	_____
_____	_____	_____
_____	_____	_____
_____	_____	_____
_____	_____	_____
_____	_____	_____
_____	_____	_____

TOTAL Debt:

Weekly "Where's My Money" Part

MONDAY: Need it?   Amount

________________________________   [Yes] [No]   ________________
________________________________   [Yes] [No]   ________________
________________________________   [Yes] [No]   ________________
________________________________   [Yes] [No]   ________________
________________________________   [Yes] [No]   ________________
________________________________   [Yes] [No]

TUESDAY: Need it?   Amount

________________________________   [Yes] [No]   ________________
________________________________   [Yes] [No]   ________________
________________________________   [Yes] [No]   ________________
________________________________   [Yes] [No]   ________________
________________________________   [Yes] [No]   ________________
________________________________   [Yes] [No]

WEDNESDAY: Need it?   Amount

________________________________   [Yes] [No]   ________________
________________________________   [Yes] [No]   ________________
________________________________   [Yes] [No]   ________________
________________________________   [Yes] [No]   ________________
________________________________   [Yes] [No]   ________________
________________________________   [Yes] [No]

EXPENSES:

INCOME   1 SOURCE: 2 SOURCE: 3 SOURCE:

THURSDAY:

	Need it?		AMOUNT
__________	Yes	No	__________
__________	Yes	No	__________
__________	Yes	No	__________
__________	Yes	No	__________
__________	Yes	No	__________
__________	Yes	No	__________

FRIDAY:

	Need it?		AMOUNT
__________	Yes	No	__________
__________	Yes	No	__________
__________	Yes	No	__________
__________	Yes	No	__________
__________	Yes	No	__________
__________	Yes	No	__________

Weekend:

	Need it?		AMOUNT
__________	Yes	No	__________
__________	Yes	No	__________
__________	Yes	No	__________
__________	Yes	No	__________
__________	Yes	No	__________
__________	Yes	No	__________

TOTAL weekly Expenses:

INCOME   4 SOURCE: 5 SOURCE: 6 SOURCE:

weekly "where's my money" part

MONDAY: Need it?   AMOUNT

	Yes	No	
	Yes	No	
	Yes	No	
	Yes	No	
	Yes	No	
	Yes	No	

TUESDAY: Need it?   AMOUNT

	Yes	No	
	Yes	No	
	Yes	No	
	Yes	No	
	Yes	No	
	Yes	No	

WEDNESDAY: Need it?   AMOUNT

	Yes	No	
	Yes	No	
	Yes	No	
	Yes	No	
	Yes	No	
	Yes	No	

EXPENSES:

INCOME   1 SOURCE: 2 SOURCE: 3 SOURCE:

THURSDAY:

Need it? AMOUNT

Yes	No
Yes	No
Yes	No
Yes	No
Yes	No
Yes	No

FRIDAY:

Need it? AMOUNT

Yes	No
Yes	No
Yes	No
Yes	No
Yes	No
Yes	No

WEEKEND:

Need it? AMOUNT

Yes	No
Yes	No
Yes	No
Yes	No
Yes	No
Yes	No

TOTAL WEEKLY EXPENSES:

INCOME   4 SOURCE: 5 SOURCE: 6 SOURCE:

weekly "where's my money" part

MONDAY: Need it?   AMOUNT

______________________________   Yes No   ____________

______________________________   Yes No   ____________

______________________________   Yes No   ____________

______________________________   Yes No   ____________

______________________________   Yes No   ____________

______________________________   Yes No   ____________

TUESDAY: Need it?   AMOUNT

______________________________   Yes No   ____________

______________________________   Yes No   ____________

______________________________   Yes No   ____________

______________________________   Yes No   ____________

______________________________   Yes No   ____________

______________________________   Yes No   ____________

WEDNESDAY: Need it?   AMOUNT

______________________________   Yes No   ____________

______________________________   Yes No   ____________

______________________________   Yes No   ____________

______________________________   Yes No   ____________

______________________________   Yes No   ____________

______________________________   Yes No   ____________

EXPENSES:

INCOME   1 SOURCE: 2 SOURCE: 3 SOURCE:

THURSDAY: Need it?   AMOUNT

	Yes	NO	
	Yes	NO	
	Yes	NO	
	Yes	NO	
	Yes	NO	
	Yes	NO	

FRIDAY: Need it?   AMOUNT

	Yes	NO	
	Yes	NO	
	Yes	NO	
	Yes	NO	
	Yes	NO	
	Yes	NO	

WEEKEND: Need it?   AMOUNT

	Yes	NO	
	Yes	NO	
	Yes	NO	
	Yes	NO	
	Yes	NO	
	Yes	NO	

TOTAL WEEKLY EXPENSES:

INCOME   4 SOURCE: 5 SOURCE: 6 SOURCE:

Weekly "Where's My Money" Part

MONDAY:

	Need it?	AMOUNT
_______________	Yes No	_______________
_______________	Yes No	
_______________	Yes No	_______________
_______________	Yes No	
_______________	Yes No	_______________
_______________	Yes No	_______________

TUESDAY:

	Need it?	AMOUNT
_______________	Yes No	_______________
_______________	Yes No	
_______________	Yes No	_______________
_______________	Yes No	
_______________	Yes No	_______________
_______________	Yes No	_______________

WEDNESDAY:

	Need it?	AMOUNT
_______________	Yes No	_______________
_______________	Yes No	
_______________	Yes No	_______________
_______________	Yes No	
_______________	Yes No	_______________
_______________	Yes No	_______________

EXPENSES:

INCOME   1 SOURCE: 2 SOURCE: 3 SOURCE:

THURSDAY:

Need it?   AMOUNT

Yes	No
Yes	No
Yes	No
Yes	No
Yes	No
Yes	No

FRIDAY:

Need it?   AMOUNT

Yes	No
Yes	No
Yes	No
Yes	No
Yes	No
Yes	No

WEEKEND:

Need it?   AMOUNT

Yes	No
Yes	No
Yes	No
Yes	No
Yes	No
Yes	No

TOTAL WEEKLY EXPENSES:

INCOME   4 SOURCE: 5 SOURCE: 6 SOURCE:

weekly "where's my money" part

MONDAY: | | Need it? | | AMOUNT

	Yes	No
Yes	No
Yes	No
Yes	No
Yes	No
Yes	No

TUESDAY: | | Need it? | | AMOUNT

	Yes	No
Yes	No
Yes	No
Yes	No
Yes	No
Yes	No

WEDNESDAY: | | Need it? | | AMOUNT

	Yes	No
Yes	No
Yes	No
Yes	No
Yes	No
Yes	No

EXPENSES:

INCOME   1 SOURCE: 2 SOURCE: 3 SOURCE:

THURSDAY:

	Need it?		AMOUNT
	Yes	No	
	Yes	No	
	Yes	No	
	Yes	No	
	Yes	No	
	Yes	No	

FRIDAY:

	Need it?		AMOUNT
	Yes	No	
	Yes	No	
	Yes	No	
	Yes	No	
	Yes	No	
	Yes	No	

WEEKEND:

	Need it?		AMOUNT
	Yes	No	
	Yes	No	
	Yes	No	
	Yes	No	
	Yes	No	
	Yes	No	

TOTAL WEEKLY EXPENSES:

INCOME   4 SOURCE: 5 SOURCE: 6 SOURCE:

WRITE SOME IMPORTANT NOTES HERE:

MONTHLY BUDGET WORKSHEET

MONTH: YEAR:

Starting
Debt

MONTHLY INCOME
1 SOURCE:
2 SOURCE:

3 SOURCE: 5 SOURCE:
4 SOURCE:
                Total:

Expenses	Spent
Rent/Mortgage	
Electric	
Water	
Phone/Cell	
Internet	
Health insurance	
Life insurance	
Car insurance	
Gas/Other transport	
Car payment	
Gifts/Books/Cosmetic	
Cloths	
Entertainment	
Eating out	
Groceries	
Utilities	
Pets	
Charity	
Unexpected	
Savings	
Total:	

MONTHLY INCOME

-

Total expenses

=

Total left to apply to debts

Debts	Applied amount	Still Owe
____	____	____
____	____	____
____	____	____
____	____	____
____	____	____
____	____	____
____	____	____
____	____	____
____	____	____
____	____	____

Total debt:

Weekly "Where's My Money" Part

MONDAY:

	Need it?		AMOUNT
_______________	Yes	No	_______
_______________	Yes	No	_______
_______________	Yes	No	_______
_______________	Yes	No	_______
_______________	Yes	No	_______
_______________	Yes	No	_______

TUESDAY:

	Need it?		AMOUNT
_______________	Yes	No	_______
_______________	Yes	No	_______
_______________	Yes	No	_______
_______________	Yes	No	_______
_______________	Yes	No	_______
_______________	Yes	No	_______

WEDNESDAY:

	Need it?		AMOUNT
_______________	Yes	No	_______
_______________	Yes	No	_______
_______________	Yes	No	_______
_______________	Yes	No	_______
_______________	Yes	No	_______
_______________	Yes	No	_______

EXPENSES:

INCOME   1 SOURCE: 2 SOURCE: 3 SOURCE:

Thursday:

	Need it?	Amount
___________	Yes No	_______
___________	Yes No	_______
___________	Yes No	_______
___________	Yes No	_______
___________	Yes No	_______
___________	Yes No	_______

Friday:

	Need it?	Amount
___________	Yes No	_______
___________	Yes No	_______
___________	Yes No	_______
___________	Yes No	_______
___________	Yes No	_______
___________	Yes No	_______

Weekend:

	Need it?	Amount
___________	Yes No	_______
___________	Yes No	_______
___________	Yes No	_______
___________	Yes No	_______
___________	Yes No	_______
___________	Yes No	_______

Total weekly Expenses:

INCOME   4 Source: 5 Source: 6 Source:

weekly "where's my money" part

MONDAY:

	Need it?		AMOUNT
_______________	Yes	No	_______________
_______________	Yes	No	_______________
_______________	Yes	No	_______________
_______________	Yes	No	_______________
_______________	Yes	No	_______________
_______________	Yes	No	_______________

Tuesday:

	Need it?		AMOUNT
_______________	Yes	No	_______________
_______________	Yes	No	_______________
_______________	Yes	No	_______________
_______________	Yes	No	_______________
_______________	Yes	No	_______________
_______________	Yes	No	_______________

Wednesday:

	Need it?		AMOUNT
_______________	Yes	No	_______________
_______________	Yes	No	_______________
_______________	Yes	No	_______________
_______________	Yes	No	_______________
_______________	Yes	No	_______________
_______________	Yes	No	_______________

Expenses:

INCOME   1 SOURCE: 2 SOURCE: 3 SOURCE:

THURSDAY: Need it?   AMOUNT

_______________________ Yes   No   _______________
_______________________ Yes   No   _______________
_______________________ Yes   No   _______________
_______________________ Yes   No   _______________
_______________________ Yes   No   _______________
_______________________ Yes   No   _______________

FRIDAY: Need it?   AMOUNT

_______________________ Yes   No   _______________
_______________________ Yes   No   _______________
_______________________ Yes   No   _______________
_______________________ Yes   No   _______________
_______________________ Yes   No   _______________
_______________________ Yes   No   _______________

Weekend: Need it?   AMOUNT

_______________________ Yes   No   _______________
_______________________ Yes   No   _______________
_______________________ Yes   No   _______________
_______________________ Yes   No   _______________
_______________________ Yes   No   _______________
_______________________ Yes   No   _______________

Total weekly Expenses:

INCOME   4 SOURCE: 5 SOURCE: 6 SOURCE:

Weekly "Where's My Money" Part

MONDAY:

Need it? AMOUNT

		Yes	No	
Yes	No
Yes	No
Yes	No
Yes	No
Yes	No

TUESDAY:

Need it? AMOUNT

Yes	No
Yes	No
Yes	No
Yes	No
Yes	No
Yes	No

WEDNESDAY:

Need it? AMOUNT

Yes	No
Yes	No
Yes	No
Yes	No
Yes	No
Yes	No

EXPENSES:

INCOME   1 SOURCE: 2 SOURCE: 3 SOURCE:

THURSDAY:

	Need it?		AMOUNT
	Yes	No	
	Yes	No	
	Yes	No	
	Yes	No	
	Yes	No	
	Yes	No	

FRIDAY:

	Need it?		AMOUNT
	Yes	No	
	Yes	No	
	Yes	No	
	Yes	No	
	Yes	No	
	Yes	No	

Weekend:

	Need it?		AMOUNT
	Yes	No	
	Yes	No	
	Yes	No	
	Yes	No	
	Yes	No	
	Yes	No	

TOTAL WEEKLY EXPENSES:

INCOME   4 SOURCE: 5 SOURCE: 6 SOURCE:

Weekly "Where's My Money" Part

MONDAY: Need it?   AMOUNT

________________________   Yes No   ____________
________________________   Yes No   ____________
________________________   Yes No   ____________
________________________   Yes No   ____________
________________________   Yes No   ____________
________________________   Yes No   ____________

TUESDAY: Need it?   AMOUNT

________________________   Yes No   ____________
________________________   Yes No   ____________
________________________   Yes No   ____________
________________________   Yes No   ____________
________________________   Yes No   ____________
________________________   Yes No   ____________

WEDNESDAY: Need it?   AMOUNT

________________________   Yes No   ____________
________________________   Yes No   ____________
________________________   Yes No   ____________
________________________   Yes No   ____________
________________________   Yes No   ____________
________________________   Yes No   ____________

EXPENSES:

INCOME   1 SOURCE: 2 SOURCE: 3 SOURCE:

THURSDAY:

Need it? AMOUNT

Yes No
Yes No
Yes No
Yes No
Yes No
Yes No

FRIDAY:

Need it? AMOUNT

Yes No
Yes No
Yes No
Yes No
Yes No
Yes No

Weekend:

Need it? AMOUNT

Yes No
Yes No
Yes No
Yes No
Yes No
Yes No

Total weekly Expenses:

INCOME 4 SOURCE: 5 SOURCE: 6 SOURCE:

Weekly "Where's My Money" Part

Monday:

	Need it?		Amount
__________________	Yes	No	__________
__________________	Yes	No	__________
__________________	Yes	No	__________
__________________	Yes	No	__________
__________________	Yes	No	__________
__________________	Yes	No	__________

Tuesday:

	Need it?		Amount
__________________	Yes	No	__________
__________________	Yes	No	__________
__________________	Yes	No	__________
__________________	Yes	No	__________
__________________	Yes	No	__________
__________________	Yes	No	__________

Wednesday:

	Need it?		Amount
__________________	Yes	No	__________
__________________	Yes	No	__________
__________________	Yes	No	__________
__________________	Yes	No	__________
__________________	Yes	No	__________
__________________	Yes	No	__________

Expenses:

Income   1 Source: 2 Source: 3 Source:

THURSDAY:

Need it?   AMOUNT

- Yes / No
- Yes / No
- Yes / No
- Yes / No
- Yes / No
- Yes / No

FRIDAY:

Need it?   AMOUNT

- Yes / No
- Yes / No
- Yes / No
- Yes / No
- Yes / No
- Yes / No

Weekend:

Need it?   AMOUNT

- Yes / No
- Yes / No
- Yes / No
- Yes / No
- Yes / No
- Yes / No

Total weekly Expenses:

INCOME   4 SOURCE: 5 SOURCE: 6 SOURCE:

Write some important Notes here:

MONTHLY BUDGET WORKSHEET

MONTH: YEAR:

Starting Debt

MONTHLY INCOME
1 SOURCE:
2 SOURCE:

3 SOURCE:
4 SOURCE:

5 SOURCE:

TOTAL:

Expenses	Spent
Rent/Mortgage	
Electric	
Water	
Phone/Cell	
Internet	
Health insurance	
Life insurance	
Car insurance	
Gas/Other transport	
Car payment	
Gifts/Books/Cosmetic	
Cloths	
Entertainment	
Eating out	
Groceries	
Utilities	
Pets	
Charity	
Unexpected	
Savings	
TOTAL:	

MONTHLY INCOME

–

TOTAL EXPENSES

=

Total left to apply to debts

Debts	Applied Amount	Still Owe
_____	_____	_____
_____	_____	_____
_____	_____	_____
_____	_____	_____
_____	_____	_____
_____	_____	_____
_____	_____	_____
_____	_____	_____
_____	_____	_____

TOTAL DEBT:

weekly "where's my money" part

MONDAY: Need it? AMOUNT

Yes	No
Yes	No
Yes	No
Yes	No
Yes	No
Yes	No

TUESDAY: Need it? AMOUNT

Yes	No
Yes	No
Yes	No
Yes	No
Yes	No
Yes	No

WEDNESDAY: Need it? AMOUNT

Yes	No
Yes	No
Yes	No
Yes	No
Yes	No
Yes	No

EXPENSES:

INCOME   1 SOURCE: 2 SOURCE: 3 SOURCE:

THURSDAY:

Need it?   AMOUNT

Yes	No
Yes	No
Yes	No
Yes	No
Yes	No
Yes	No

FRIDAY:

Need it?   AMOUNT

Yes	No
Yes	No
Yes	No
Yes	No
Yes	No
Yes	No

WeekenD:

Need it?   AMOUNT

Yes	No
Yes	No
Yes	No
Yes	No
Yes	No
Yes	No

Total weekly Expenses:

INCOME   4 SOURCE: 5 SOURCE: 6 SOURCE:

weekly "where's my money" part

MONDAY: Need it?   AMOUNT

	Need it?		Amount
	Yes	No	
	Yes	No	
	Yes	No	
	Yes	No	
	Yes	No	
	Yes	No	

TUESDAY: Need it?   AMOUNT

	Need it?		Amount
	Yes	No	
	Yes	No	
	Yes	No	
	Yes	No	
	Yes	No	
	Yes	No	

WEDNESDAY: Need it?   AMOUNT

	Need it?		Amount
	Yes	No	
	Yes	No	
	Yes	No	
	Yes	No	
	Yes	No	
	Yes	No	

EXPENSES:

INCOME   1 SOURCE: 2 SOURCE: 3 SOURCE:

THURSDAY:

Need it?   AMOUNT

Yes	No
Yes	No
Yes	No
Yes	No
Yes	No
Yes	No

FRIDAY:

Need it?   AMOUNT

Yes	No
Yes	No
Yes	No
Yes	No
Yes	No
Yes	No

Weekend:

Need it?   AMOUNT

Yes	No
Yes	No
Yes	No
Yes	No
Yes	No
Yes	No

TOTAL WEEKLY EXPENSES:

INCOME   4 SOURCE: 5 SOURCE: 6 SOURCE:

weekly "where's my money" part

MONDAY: Need it?   AMOUNT

	Yes	No	
	Yes	No	
	Yes	No	
	Yes	No	
	Yes	No	
	Yes	No	

TUESDAY: Need it?   AMOUNT

	Yes	No	
	Yes	No	
	Yes	No	
	Yes	No	
	Yes	No	
	Yes	No	

WEDNESDAY: Need it?   AMOUNT

	Yes	No	
	Yes	No	
	Yes	No	
	Yes	No	
	Yes	No	
	Yes	No	

EXPENSES:

INCOME   1 SOURCE: 2 SOURCE: 3 SOURCE:

Thursday: Need it? Amount

Yes	No
Yes	No
Yes	No
Yes	No
Yes	No
Yes	No

Friday: Need it? Amount

Yes	No
Yes	No
Yes	No
Yes	No
Yes	No
Yes	No

Weekend: Need it? Amount

Yes	No
Yes	No
Yes	No
Yes	No
Yes	No
Yes	No

Total weekly Expenses:

Income   4 Source: 5 Source: 6 Source:

weekly "where's my money" part

MONDAY: Need it?   AMOUNT

Yes	No
Yes	No
Yes	No
Yes	No
Yes	No
Yes	No

TUESDAY: Need it?   AMOUNT

Yes	No
Yes	No
Yes	No
Yes	No
Yes	No
Yes	No

WEDNESDAY: Need it?   AMOUNT

Yes	No
Yes	No
Yes	No
Yes	No
Yes	No
Yes	No

EXPENSES:

INCOME   1 SOURCE: 2 SOURCE: 3 SOURCE:

THURSDAY:

Need it?   AMOUNT

Yes	NO
Yes	NO
Yes	NO
Yes	NO
Yes	NO
Yes	NO

FRIDAY:

Need it?   AMOUNT

Yes	NO
Yes	NO
Yes	NO
Yes	NO
Yes	NO
Yes	NO

WEEKEND:

Need it?   AMOUNT

Yes	NO
Yes	NO
Yes	NO
Yes	NO
Yes	NO
Yes	NO

TOTAL WEEKLY EXPENSES:

INCOME   4 SOURCE: 5 SOURCE: 6 SOURCE:

weekly "where's my money" Part

MONDAY:

	Need it?	AMOUNT
	Yes / No	
	Yes / No	
	Yes / No	
	Yes / No	
	Yes / No	
	Yes / No	

TUESDAY:

	Need it?	AMOUNT
	Yes / No	
	Yes / No	
	Yes / No	
	Yes / No	
	Yes / No	
	Yes / No	

WEDNESDAY:

	Need it?	AMOUNT
	Yes / No	
	Yes / No	
	Yes / No	
	Yes / No	
	Yes / No	
	Yes / No	

EXPENSES:

INCOME　　1 SOURCE:　　2 SOURCE:　　3 SOURCE:

THURSDAY:

Need it?   **AMOUNT**

______________________   [Yes] [No]
______________________   [Yes] [No]
______________________   [Yes] [No]
______________________   [Yes] [No]
______________________   [Yes] [No]
______________________   [Yes] [No]

FRIDAY:

Need it?   **AMOUNT**

______________________   [Yes] [No]
______________________   [Yes] [No]
______________________   [Yes] [No]
______________________   [Yes] [No]
______________________   [Yes] [No]
______________________   [Yes] [No]

WEEKEND:

Need it?   **AMOUNT**

______________________   [Yes] [No]
______________________   [Yes] [No]
______________________   [Yes] [No]
______________________   [Yes] [No]
______________________   [Yes] [No]
______________________   [Yes] [No]

TOTAL WEEKLY EXPENSES:

INCOME   4 SOURCE: 5 SOURCE: 6 SOURCE:

WRITE SOME IMPORTANT NOTES HERE:

MONTHLY BUDGET WORKSHEET

MONTH: YEAR:

Starting debt

MONTHLY INCOME
1 SOURCE:
2 SOURCE:

3 SOURCE: 5 SOURCE:
4 SOURCE:

TOTAL:

Expenses	Spent
Rent/Mortgage	
Electric	
Water	
Phone/Cell	
Internet	
Health insurance	
Life insurance	
Car insurance	
Gas/Other transport	
Car payment	
Gifts/Books/Cosmetic	
Cloths	
Entertainment	
Eating out	
Groceries	
Utilities	
Pets	
Charity	
Unexpected	
Savings	
TOTAL:	

MONTHLY INCOME

-

TOTAL expenses

=

Total left to apply to debts

Debts	Applied Amount	Still Owe

TOTAL debt:

weekly "where's my money" part

MONDAY:

	Need it?		AMOUNT
	Yes	No	
	Yes	No	
	Yes	No	
	Yes	No	
	Yes	No	
	Yes	No	

Tuesday:

	Need it?		AMOUNT
	Yes	No	
	Yes	No	
	Yes	No	
	Yes	No	
	Yes	No	
	Yes	No	

Wednesday:

	Need it?		AMOUNT
	Yes	No	
	Yes	No	
	Yes	No	
	Yes	No	
	Yes	No	
	Yes	No	

EXPENSES:

INCOME   1 SOURCE: 2 SOURCE: 3 SOURCE:

THURSDAY:

	Need it?		AMOUNT
	Yes	No	
	Yes	No	
	Yes	No	
	Yes	No	
	Yes	No	
	Yes	No	

FRIDAY:

	Need it?		AMOUNT
	Yes	No	
	Yes	No	
	Yes	No	
	Yes	No	
	Yes	No	
	Yes	No	

Weekend:

	Need it?		AMOUNT
	Yes	No	
	Yes	No	
	Yes	No	
	Yes	No	
	Yes	No	
	Yes	No	

Total weekly Expenses:

INCOME   4 SOURCE: 5 SOURCE: 6 SOURCE:

weekly "where's my money" part

MONDAY:

	Need it?		AMOUNT
	Yes	No	
	Yes	No	
	Yes	No	
	Yes	No	
	Yes	No	
	Yes	No	

Tuesday:

	Need it?		AMOUNT
	Yes	No	
	Yes	No	
	Yes	No	
	Yes	No	
	Yes	No	
	Yes	No	

Wednesday:

	Need it?		AMOUNT
	Yes	No	
	Yes	No	
	Yes	No	
	Yes	No	
	Yes	No	
	Yes	No	

Expenses:

INCOME   1 SOURCE: 2 SOURCE: 3 SOURCE:

THURSDAY:

	Need it?		AMOUNT
_____________________	Yes	No	_______
_____________________	Yes	No	_______
_____________________	Yes	No	_______
_____________________	Yes	No	_______
_____________________	Yes	No	_______
_____________________	Yes	No	_______

FRIDAY:

	Need it?		AMOUNT
_____________________	Yes	No	_______
_____________________	Yes	No	_______
_____________________	Yes	No	_______
_____________________	Yes	No	_______
_____________________	Yes	No	_______
_____________________	Yes	No	_______

Weekend:

	Need it?		AMOUNT
_____________________	Yes	No	_______
_____________________	Yes	No	_______
_____________________	Yes	No	_______
_____________________	Yes	No	_______
_____________________	Yes	No	_______
_____________________	Yes	No	_______

Total weekly Expenses:

INCOME   4 SOURCE: 5 SOURCE: 6 SOURCE:

Weekly "Where's My Money" Part

MONDAY:

	Need it?		AMOUNT
___________________________	Yes	No	_________
___________________________	Yes	No	_________
___________________________	Yes	No	_________
___________________________	Yes	No	_________
___________________________	Yes	No	_________
___________________________	Yes	No	_________

TUESDAY:

	Need it?		AMOUNT
___________________________	Yes	No	_________
___________________________	Yes	No	_________
___________________________	Yes	No	_________
___________________________	Yes	No	_________
___________________________	Yes	No	_________
___________________________	Yes	No	_________

WEDNESDAY:

	Need it?		AMOUNT
___________________________	Yes	No	_________
___________________________	Yes	No	_________
___________________________	Yes	No	_________
___________________________	Yes	No	_________
___________________________	Yes	No	_________
___________________________	Yes	No	_________

EXPENSES:

INCOME   1 SOURCE: 2 SOURCE: 3 SOURCE:

THURSDAY: Need it?   AMOUNT

	Yes	No
	Yes	No
	Yes	No
	Yes	No
	Yes	No
	Yes	No

FRIDAY: Need it?   AMOUNT

	Yes	No
	Yes	No
	Yes	No
	Yes	No
	Yes	No
	Yes	No

Weekend: Need it?   AMOUNT

	Yes	No
	Yes	No
	Yes	No
	Yes	No
	Yes	No
	Yes	No

TOTAL weekly Expenses:

INCOME   4 SOURCE: 5 SOURCE: 6 SOURCE:

weekly "where's my money" part

MONDAY:

	Need it?		AMOUNT
____________________	Yes	No	__________
____________________	Yes	No	__________
____________________	Yes	No	__________
____________________	Yes	No	__________
____________________	Yes	No	__________
____________________	Yes	No	__________

TUESDAY:

	Need it?		AMOUNT
____________________	Yes	No	__________
____________________	Yes	No	__________
____________________	Yes	No	__________
____________________	Yes	No	__________
____________________	Yes	No	__________
____________________	Yes	No	__________

WEDNESDAY:

	Need it?		AMOUNT
____________________	Yes	No	__________
____________________	Yes	No	__________
____________________	Yes	No	__________
____________________	Yes	No	__________
____________________	Yes	No	__________
____________________	Yes	No	__________

EXPENSES:

INCOME   1 SOURCE: 2 SOURCE: 3 SOURCE:

THURSDAY:

	Need it?		AMOUNT
___________________	Yes	No	__________
___________________	Yes	No	__________
___________________	Yes	No	__________
___________________	Yes	No	__________
___________________	Yes	No	__________
___________________	Yes	No	__________

FRiday:

	Need it?		AMOUNT
___________________	Yes	No	__________
___________________	Yes	No	__________
___________________	Yes	No	__________
___________________	Yes	No	__________
___________________	Yes	No	__________
___________________	Yes	No	__________

Weekend:

	Need it?		AMOUNT
___________________	Yes	No	__________
___________________	Yes	No	__________
___________________	Yes	No	__________
___________________	Yes	No	__________
___________________	Yes	No	__________
___________________	Yes	No	__________

Total weekly Expenses:

INCOME   4 SOURCE: 5 SOURCE: 6 SOURCE:

weekly "where's my money" part

MONDAY: Need it?   AMOUNT

___________________________________   [Yes] [No]   ___________________

___________________________________   [Yes] [No]   ___________________

___________________________________   [Yes] [No]   ___________________

___________________________________   [Yes] [No]   ___________________

___________________________________   [Yes] [No]   ___________________

                                              [Yes] [No]   ___________________

Tuesday: Need it?   AMOUNT

___________________________________   [Yes] [No]   ___________________

___________________________________   [Yes] [No]   ___________________

___________________________________   [Yes] [No]   ___________________

___________________________________   [Yes] [No]   ___________________

___________________________________   [Yes] [No]   ___________________

                                              [Yes] [No]   ___________________

Wednesday: Need it?   AMOUNT

___________________________________   [Yes] [No]   ___________________

___________________________________   [Yes] [No]   ___________________

___________________________________   [Yes] [No]   ___________________

___________________________________   [Yes] [No]   ___________________

___________________________________   [Yes] [No]   ___________________

                                              [Yes] [No]   ___________________

EXPenses:

INCOME   1 SOURCE: 2 SOURCE: 3 SOURCE:

THURSDAY:

	Need it?	Amount
_______________	Yes / No	_______________
_______________	Yes / No	_______________
_______________	Yes / No	_______________
_______________	Yes / No	_______________
_______________	Yes / No	_______________
_______________	Yes / No	_______________

FRIDAY:

	Need it?	Amount
_______________	Yes / No	_______________
_______________	Yes / No	_______________
_______________	Yes / No	_______________
_______________	Yes / No	_______________
_______________	Yes / No	_______________
_______________	Yes / No	_______________

Weekend:

	Need it?	Amount
_______________	Yes / No	_______________
_______________	Yes / No	_______________
_______________	Yes / No	_______________
_______________	Yes / No	_______________
_______________	Yes / No	_______________
_______________	Yes / No	_______________

Total weekly Expenses:

INCOME   4 SOURCE: 5 SOURCE: 6 SOURCE:

WRite some importaNt Notes Here:

Write some important Notes here:

WRITE SOME IMPORTANT NOTES HERE:

WRITE SOME IMPORTANT NOTES HERE:

Write some important Notes here:

WRITE SOME IMPORTANT NOTES HERE:

Write some important Notes here:

WRITE SOME IMPORTANT NOTES HERE:

WRITE SOME IMPORTANT NOTES HERE:

WRITE SOME IMPORTANT NOTES HERE:

Write some important Notes here:

WRITE SOME IMPORTANT NOTES HERE:

WRITE SOME IMPORTANT NOTES HERE:

WRITE SOME IMPORTANT NOTES HERE:

Did you make it up to here?

You are G.O.A.T.

(greatest of all time)